Position Pieces
for Cello

by Rick Mooney

Book Two

© 2003 Summy-Birchard Music
a division of Summy-Birchard Inc.
Exclusive print rights administered by Alfred Music
All rights reserved. Printed in USA
ISBN 10: 1-5895-1205-7   ISBN 13: 978-1-5895-1205-4

T0054309

Contents

Introduction

This book deals with Fifth, Sixth and Seventh positions on the cello. Coincidentally, because of the range of the notes commonly used in those positions, there is a lot of practice reading tenor clef. It is assumed that the student is already familiar with First through Fourth positions. Those positions are used in this book but not presented in a systematic manner. For that I refer you to the first book of *Position Pieces for Cello*.

The way this book deals with these "three finger positions" is different from the traditional approach in a couple of ways:

I have used the Target system introduced in the first book of *Position Pieces* to find the correct place on the fingerboard. The notes that I use as Targets can be tested against open strings and harmonics for accurate intonation. That helps students to practice correctly at home. Thus I have defined Fifth Position as 2nd finger on G on the A-string rather than the traditional definition of 1st finger on F because G can be tested and F cannot. You will notice that this does not actually contradict the traditional definition. Mainly, it is a different way of thinking about it.

When possible, I prefer to find the Target with 2nd finger rather than 1st. I think this helps to set up the balance of the hand so it is easier to find the placement of all the other fingers. Thus I have defined Sixth Position as 2nd finger on A on the A-string. Of course there is an overlap here and some of these pieces do utilize 1st finger on G on the A-string to find Sixth position. But I use the 2nd finger Target to define the various finger patterns mentioned below.

I have specifically defined the three main finger patterns used in this part of the fingerboard. I have numbered them based on the numbering system used in *Thumb Position for Cello*. Pattern I consists of a whole step between 1st and 2nd fingers, with a half step between 2nd and 3rd fingers. Pattern II is a half step between 1st and 2nd then a whole step between 2nd and 3rd. Pattern III is all whole steps. This represents a continuation of the fundamental concept presented in my other books. In order to find any particular group of notes on the cello we must have two pieces of information: the Target and the distance between the neighboring notes.

Because I have limited this book to the three main finger patterns, you will notice that there are some patterns and certain specific groups of notes that are not used. My goal was to present a practical system of playing in these positions without necessarily being exhaustive with all conceivable situations. I think that the system described above (finding the Targets and intervals) can be used just as effectively to deal with the more "exceptional" patterns. However, be on the lookout for the Chromatic Pattern (all half steps). I have sneaked it into a couple of the pieces as a little surprise!

As with the first book of *Position Pieces*, the student should play the top line of the duets. The fingerings are also used the same way: I always put in a fingering if you have to shift. So if you do *not* see a fingering that means you do *not* have to shift and you must figure out how to play the note(s) without moving your hand. (You will also notice that I did not thoroughly mark the bottom line, which is intended for the teacher. If you have students playing that line, you may find it necessary to add fingerings.)

As a general rule throughout this book I decided not to indicate the bow direction to be used at the beginning of pieces. At a certain point in time I think it is important for students to know that if a piece begins on a down beat, you play it with a down bow and if it begins on an up beat, you play it with an up bow. If for any reason that is not the case, there will be a specific bowing notation to follow. So I left out those bowing indications unless they were necessary for clarification (like down bow re-takes on repeats).

Finally I would like to mention the words you will see in a few of the pieces. These were never actually intended to be songs. In fact you will notice that no consideration has been given to a normal vocal range. It is just that once in a while lyrics occurred to me as I was working on a piece. I decided to include them in the hope that they will enhance your enjoyment of the music.

I hope you have as much fun playing these pieces as I had writing them!

Rick Mooney

Fifth Position Warm-ups

Target Practice

Fifth Position Warm-ups continued

Note: Play this on the G and C strings also

Note: Play this on the G and C strings also

Fifth Position Pattern I

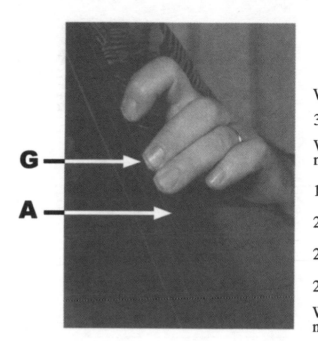

Geography Quiz

Your 2nd finger is on G on the A-string.
Answer the following questions:

What note will be played by:

3 on the A-string? _____

What is another
name for that note? _____

1 on the A-string? _____

2 on the D-string? _____

2 on the G-string? _____

2 on the C-string? _____

What is another
name for that note? _____

What finger will you use to play:

C♯ on the D-string? _____

E♭ on the G-string? _____

F♯ on the G-string? _____

B on the C-string? _____

G♯ on the C-string? _____

B♭ on the D-string? _____

G♯ on the A-string? _____

Names and Numbers

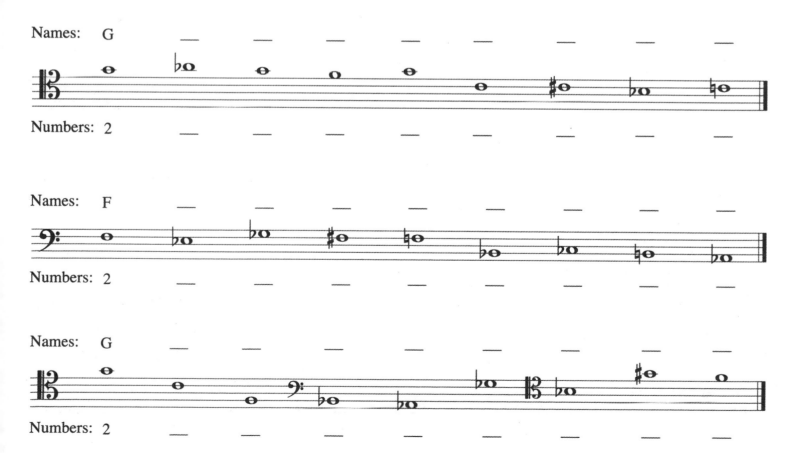

Fifth Position Pattern I

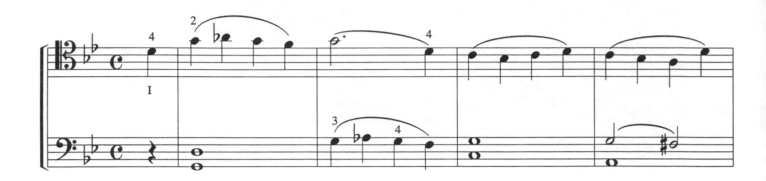

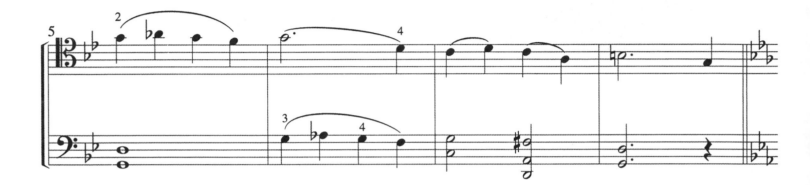

Fifth Position Pattern I

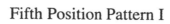

Legend

Legend

March of the Gladiators

Fine

D. C. al Fine

Fifth Position Pattern II

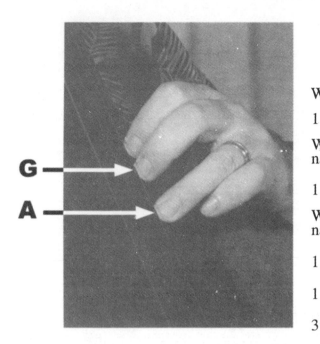

G →
A →

Geography Quiz

Your 2nd finger is on G on the A-string.
Answer the following questions:

What note will be played by:

1 on the A-string? _____

What is another
name for that note? _____

1 on the D-string? _____

What is another
name for that note? _____

1 on the G-string? _____

1 on the C-string? _____

3 on the C-string? _____

What finger will you use to play:

D on the D-string? _____

C on the D-string? _____

F on the G-string? _____

B♭ on the C-string? _____

A on the A-string? _____

A on the C-string? _____

G on the G-string? _____

Names and Numbers

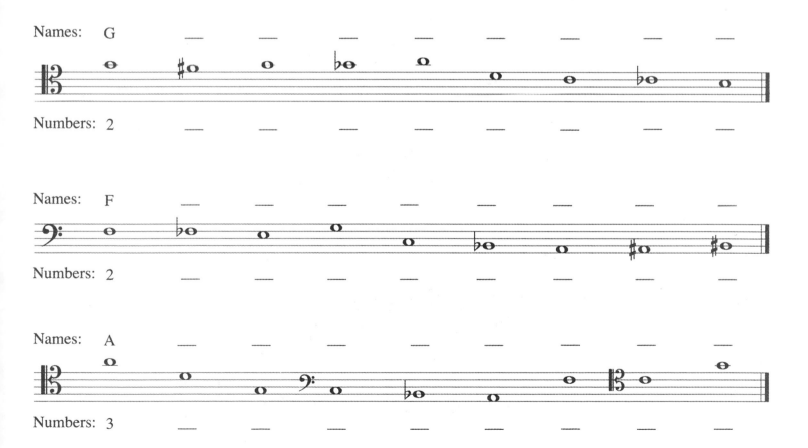

Names: G   __   __   __   __   __   __   __   __   __

Numbers: 2   __   __   __   __   __   __   __   __   __

Names: F   __   __   __   __   __   __   __   __   __

Numbers: 2   __   __   __   __   __   __   __   __   __

Names: A   __   __   __   __   __   __   __   __   __

Numbers: 3   __   __   __   __   __   __   __   __   __

Fifth Position Pattern II

Fifth Position Pattern II

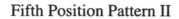

Spanish Serenade

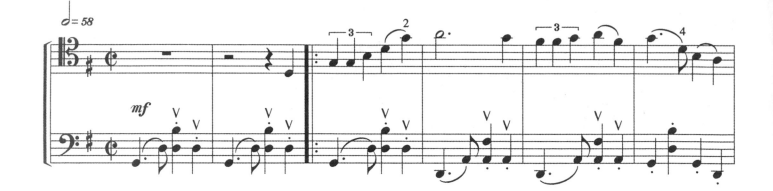

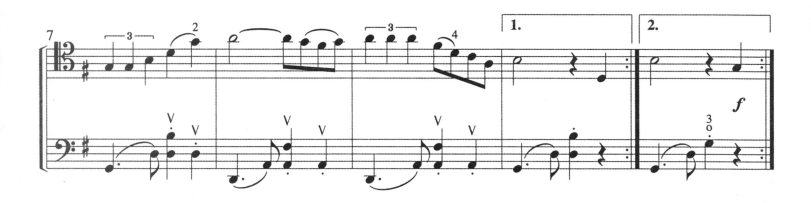

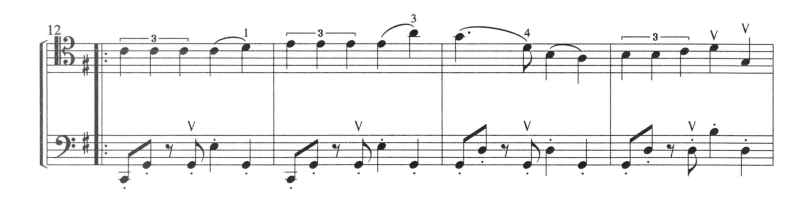

Spanish Serenade

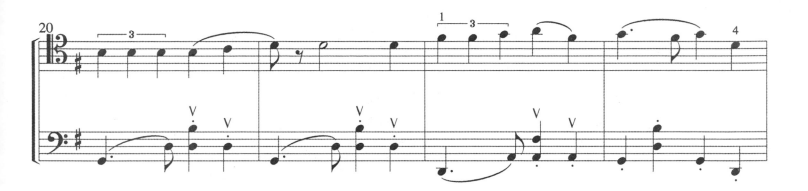

Boogie March

D. S. al Fine

Fifth Position Pattern III

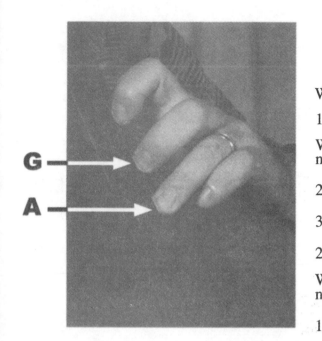

Geography Quiz

Your 2nd finger is on G on the A-string.
Answer the following questions:

What note will be played by:

1 on the D-string? _____

What is another
name for that note? _____

2 on the G-string? _____

3 on the G-string? _____

2 on the C-string? _____

What is another
name for that note? _____

1 on the A-string? _____

What finger will you use to play:

A on the A-string? _____

C on the D-string? _____

Eb on the G-string? _____

Ab on the C-string? _____

D♯ on the G-string? _____

D on the D-string? _____

C on the C-string? _____

Names and Numbers

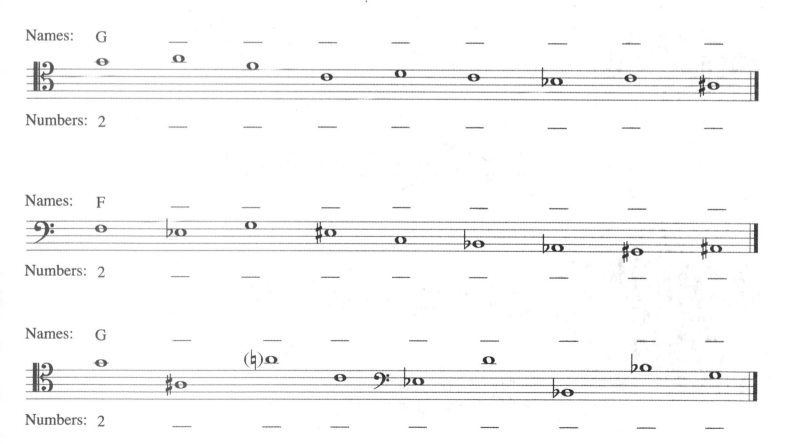

Fifth Position Pattern III

Fifth Position Pattern III

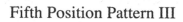

Moon Over the Ruined Trailer Park

Moon Over the Ruined Trailer Park

Exercise in Facility

Fine

D. C. al Fine

Upper Fifth Position

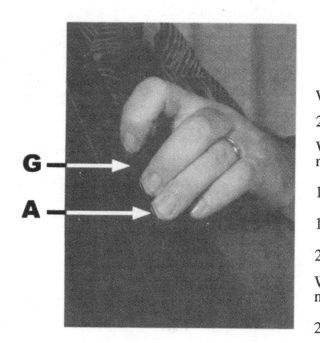

G →
A →

Geography Quiz

Your 3rd finger is on A on the A-string.
Answer the following questions:

What note will be played by:

2 on the A-string? _____

What is another
name for that note? _____

1 on the D-string? _____

1 on the G-string? _____

2 on the D-string? _____

What is another
name for that note? _____

2 on the C-string? _____

What finger will you use to play:

F♯ on the A-string? _____

E on the G-string? _____

A on the C-string? _____

F♯ on the G-string? _____

D♭ on the D-string? _____

G on the G-string? _____

C on the C-string? _____

Names and Numbers

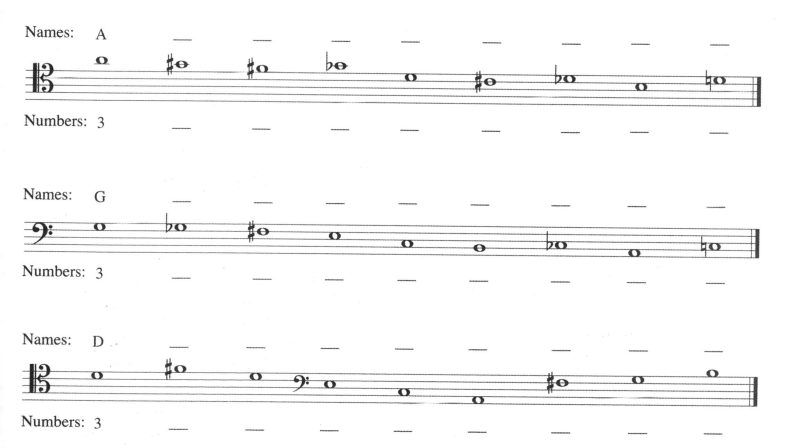

Names: A ___ ___ ___ ___ ___ ___ ___ ___

Numbers: 3 ___ ___ ___ ___ ___ ___ ___ ___

Names: G ___ ___ ___ ___ ___ ___ ___ ___

Numbers: 3 ___ ___ ___ ___ ___ ___ ___ ___

Names: D ___ ___ ___ ___ ___ ___ ___ ___

Numbers: 3 ___ ___ ___ ___ ___ ___ ___ ___

Upper Fifth Position

Upper Fifth Position

A Little Song

Fine

D. S. al Fine

The Happy Certified Public Accountant

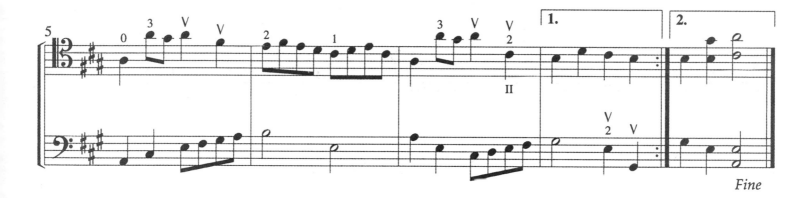

Rollicking Rondo

Rollicking Rondo

D. S. al Fine

Succinct Sonata

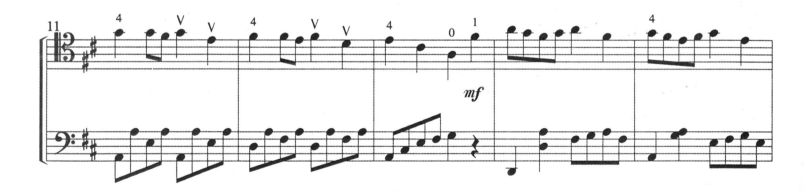

Succinct Sonata

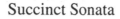

Fine

D. S. al Fine

Chant

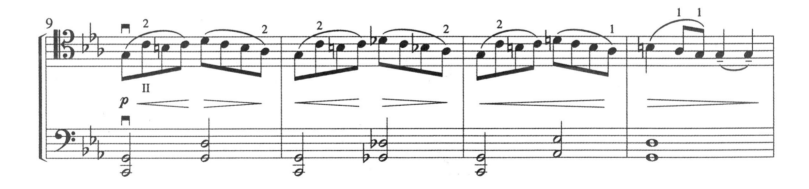

D. C. al Fine

Sixth Position Warm-ups

Target Practice

Pattern I

Sixth Position Warm-ups continued

Note: Play this on the G and C strings also

Note: Play this on the G and C strings also

Sixth Position Pattern I

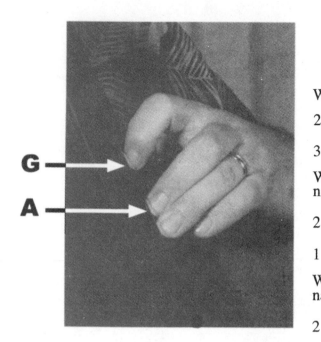

G →

A →

Geography Quiz

Your 2nd finger is on A on the A-string.
Answer the following questions:

What note will be played by:

2 on the D-string? _____

3 on the A-string? _____

What is another
name for that note? _____

2 on the C-string? _____

1 on the C-string? _____

What is another
name for that note? _____

2 on the G-string? _____

What finger will you use to play:

A♭ on the G-string? _____

G on the A-string? _____

D♯ on the D-string? _____

E♭ on the D-string? _____

C on the C-string? _____

F on the G-string? _____

C on the D-string? _____

Names and Numbers

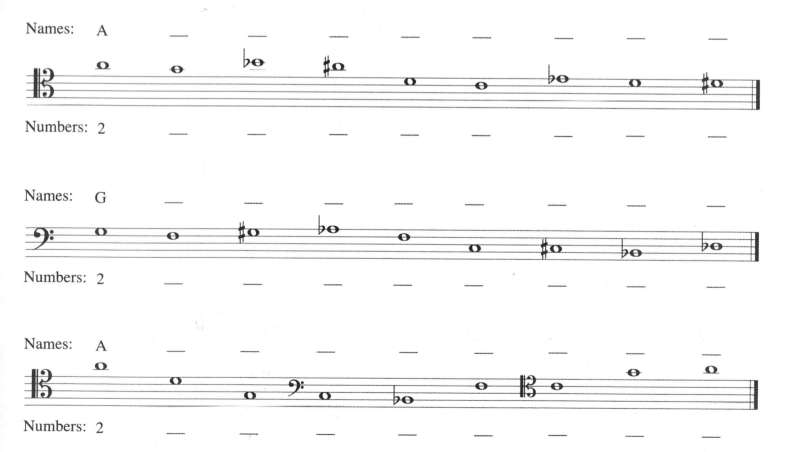

Names: A __ __ __ __ __ __ __ __

Numbers: 2 __ __ __ __ __ __ __ __

Names: G __ __ __ __ __ __ __ __

Numbers: 2 __ __ __ __ __ __ __ __

Names: A __ __ __ __ __ __ __ __

Numbers: 2 __ __ __ __ __ __ __ __

Sixth Position Pattern I

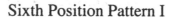

Sixth Position Pattern I

Lullaby

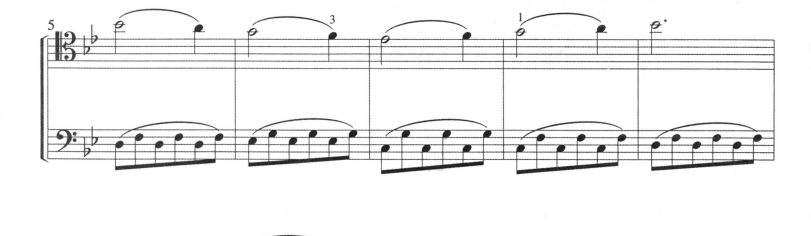

Lullaby

Wistful Waltz

Sixth Position Pattern II

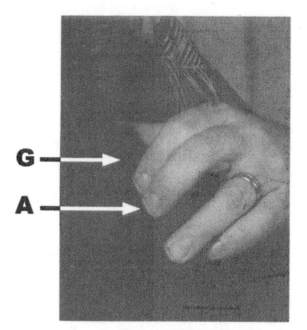

Geography Quiz
Your 2nd finger is on A on the A-string.
Answer the following questions:

What note will be played by:

1 on the A-string? _____

What is another
name for that note? _____

3 on the A-string? _____

2 on the D-string? _____

1 on the G-string? _____

What is another
name for that note? _____

2 on the C-string? _____

What finger will you use to play:

D on the C-string? _____

B on the C-string? _____

E on the D-string? _____

G on the G-string? _____

F# on the G-string? _____

C# on the D-string? _____

A on the G-string? _____

Names and Numbers

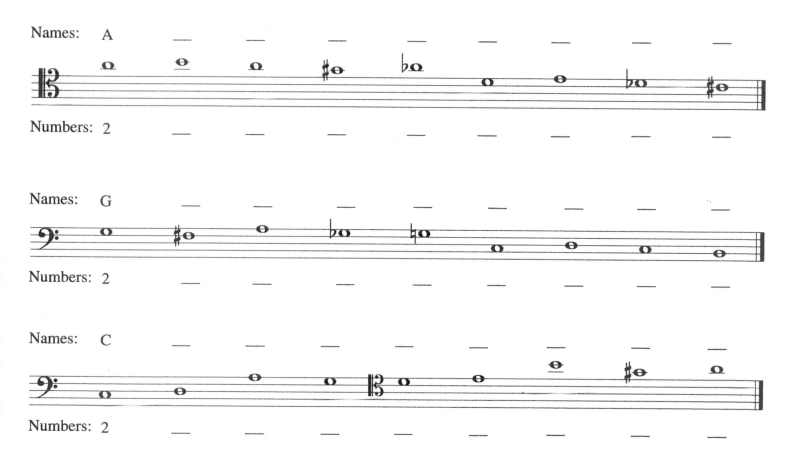

Sixth Position Pattern II

Sixth Position Pattern II

A Major March

A Major March

Gondola Song

Sixth Position Pattern III

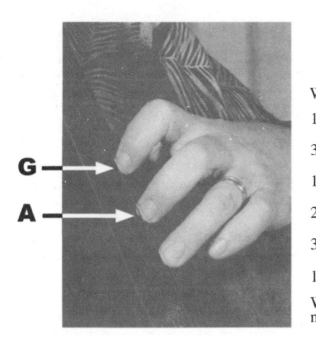

G →
A →

Geography Quiz

Your 2nd finger is on A on the A-string.
Answer the following questions:

What note will be played by:

1 on the D-string? _____

3 on the A-string? _____

1 on the A-string? _____

2 on the G-string? _____

3 on the G-string? _____

1 on the C-string? _____

What is another
name for that note? _____

What finger will you use to play:

C on the C-string? _____

G on the A-string? _____

E on the D-string? _____

D on the C-string? _____

F on the G-string? _____

D on the D-string? _____

B on the A-string? _____

Names and Numbers

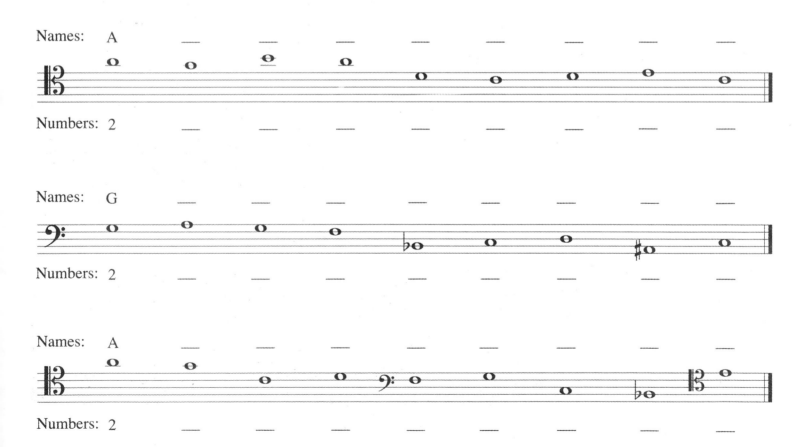

Names: A   __   __   __   __   __   __   __   __

Numbers: 2   __   __   __   __   __   __   __   __

Names: G   __   __   __   __   __   __   __   __

Numbers: 2   __   __   __   __   __   __   __   __

Names: A   __   __   __   __   __   __   __   __

Numbers: 2   __   __   __   __   __   __   __   __

Sixth Position Pattern III

Sixth Position Pattern III

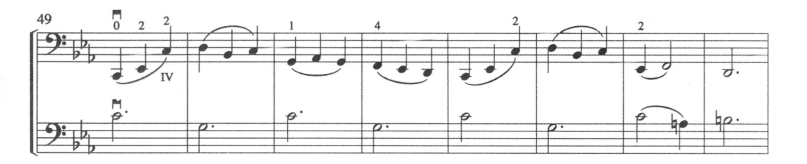

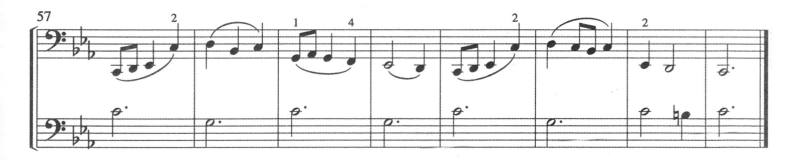

52

Ballad

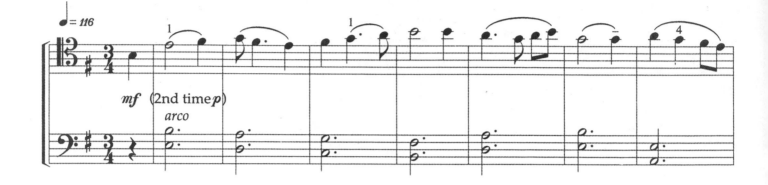

Ballad

D. C. al Fine

The Lonesome Cowboy

The Lonesome Cowboy

they   like to stand up - wind!   *mf* I'm at-tract-ing

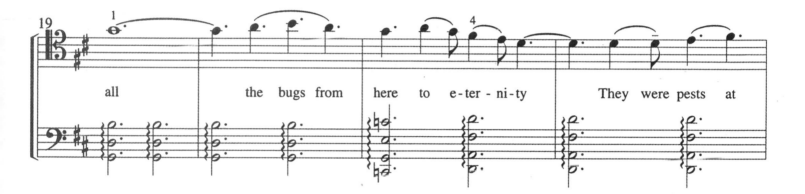

all   the bugs from   here to e-ter-ni-ty   They were pests at

first   but then it oc-curred to me   when I'm on the   trail

I real-ly   do like the com-pa-ny   and in man-y   ways

56

The Lonesome Cowboy

my lit-tle friends are good for me: When the clouds of bugs

are all thick and black, I can in - hale

a bet-ween meal snack! A

tas - ty bet - we - en meal snack!

Lower Sixth Position

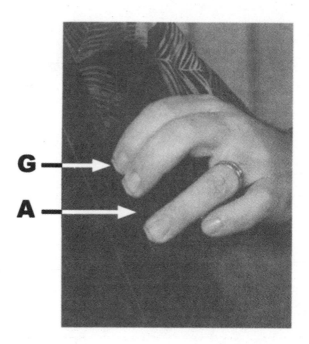

Geography Quiz

Your 1st finger is on G on the A-string.
Answer the following questions:

What note will be played by:

1 on the D-string? _____

2 on the A-string? _____

What is another
name for that note? _____

2 on the G-string? _____

2 on the C-string? _____

3 on the D-string? _____

What is another
name for that note? _____

What finger will you use to play:

B♭ on the A-string? _____

C♯ on the D-string? _____

F on the G-string? _____

B♭ on the C-string? _____

G on the A-string? _____

C♯ on the C-string? _____

G♯ on the G-string? _____

Names and Numbers

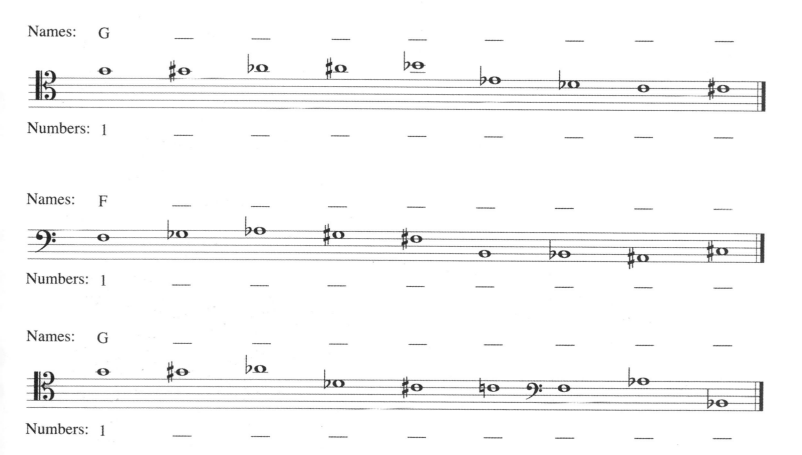

58

Lower Sixth Position

Lower Sixth Position

Sicilienne

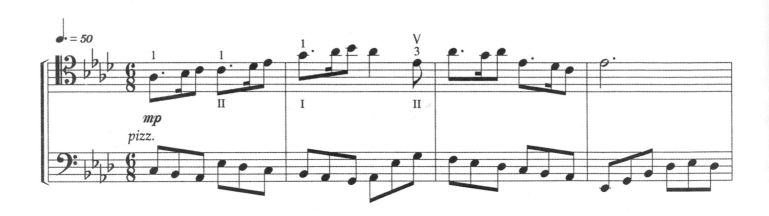

Fine

D. C. al Fine

Soliloquy

If I were Yo Yo Ma, I'd play with-out a flaw. I

won - der how he does all that, 'cause I've lost B - flat! I

played it yes-ter - day. It's right next door to "A". But

now I real-ly don't know when I'll find_____it a - gain.

Dialogue

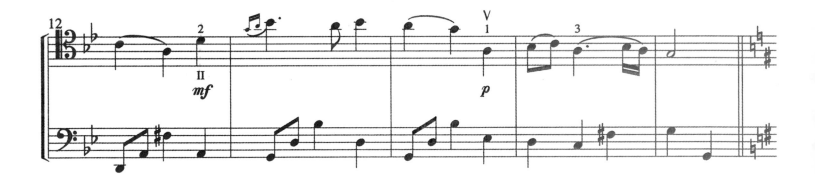

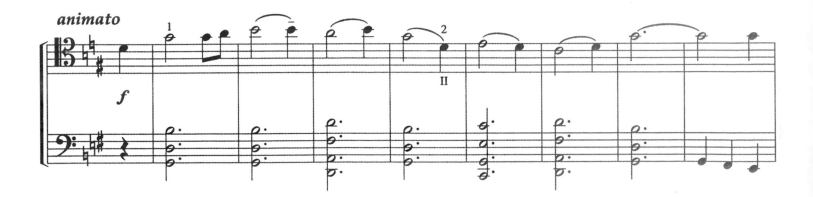

Dialogue

Tempo I

Old Air

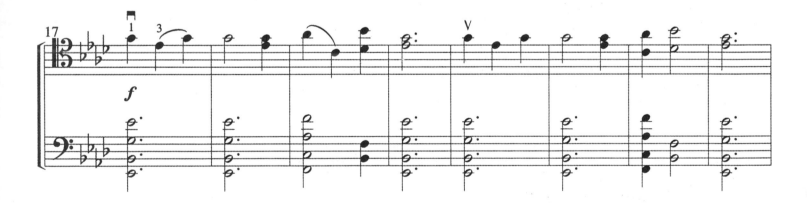

Old Air

The Mime

Fine

D. C. al Fine

Seventh Position Warm-ups

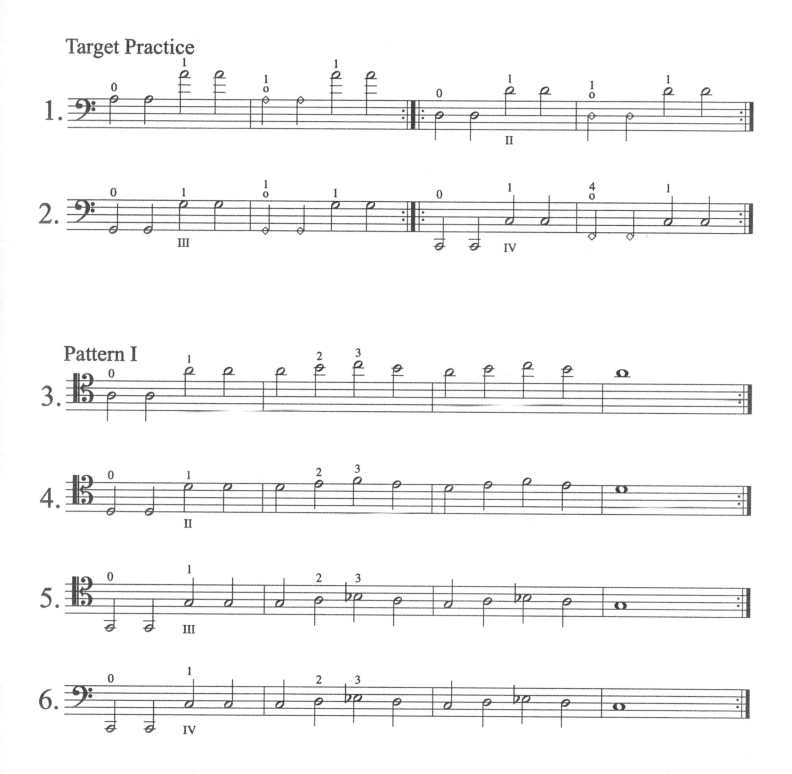

Seventh Position Warm-ups continued

Seventh Position Pattern I

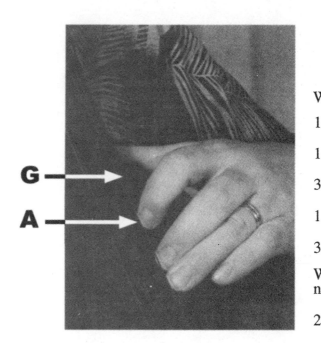

Geography Quiz

Your 1st finger is on A on the A-string.
Answer the following questions:

What note will be played by:

1 on the G-string? _____

1 on the C-string? _____

3 on the A-string? _____

1 on the D-string? _____

3 on the G-string? _____

What is another
name for that note? _____

2 on the A-string? _____

What finger will you use to play:

B on the A-string? _____

F on the D-string? _____

E on the D-string? _____

A on the G-string? _____

B♭ on the G-string? _____

D on the C-string? _____

E♭ on the C-string? _____

Names and Numbers

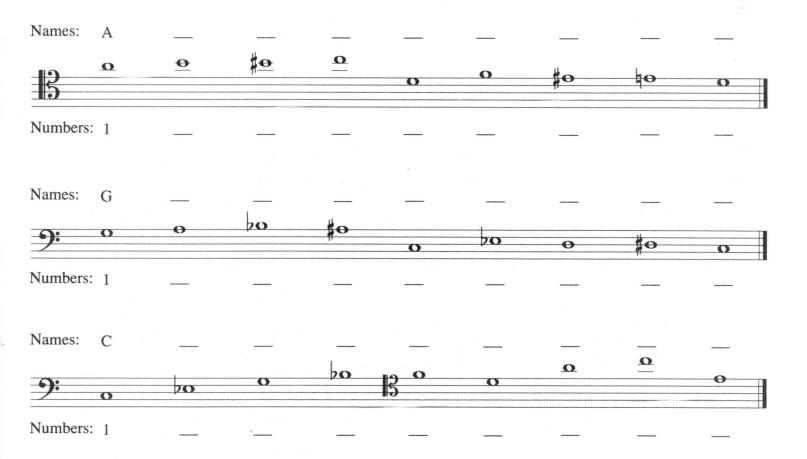

Names: A   ___   ___   ___   ___   ___   ___   ___   ___

Numbers: 1   ___   ___   ___   ___   ___   ___   ___   ___

Names: G   ___   ___   ___   ___   ___   ___   ___   ___

Numbers: 1   ___   ___   ___   ___   ___   ___   ___   ___

Names: C   ___   ___   ___   ___   ___   ___   ___   ___

Numbers: 1   ___   ___   ___   ___   ___   ___   ___   ___

Seventh Position Pattern I

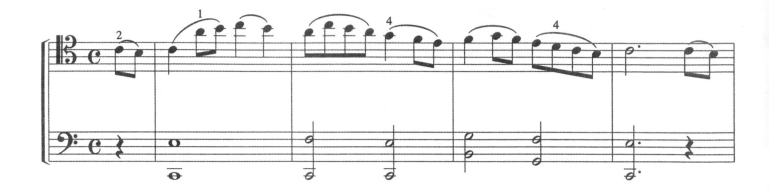

Seventh Position Pattern I

Russian Song

Russian Song

Hungarian Dance

Seventh Position Pattern II

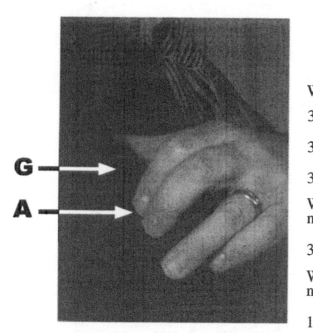

G →

A →

Geography Quiz

Your 1st finger is on A on the A-string.
Answer the following questions:

What note will be played by:

3 on the A-string? _____

3 on the D-string? _____

3 on the G-string? _____

What is another
name for that note? _____

3 on the C-string? _____

What is another
name for that note? _____

1 on the G-string? _____

What finger will you use to play:

B♭ on the A-string? _____

E♭ on the D-string? _____

A♭ on the G-string? _____

C♯ on the C-string? _____

D on the D-string? _____

B♭ on the G-string? _____

A♯ on the A-string? _____

Names and Numbers

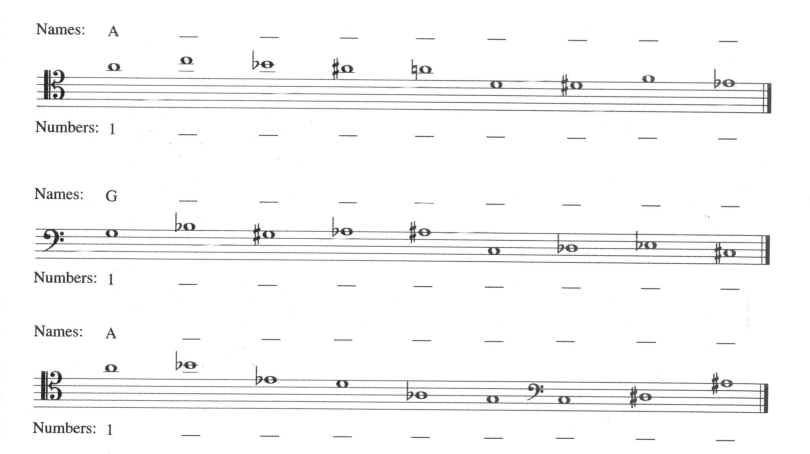

Names: A   __   __   __   __   __   __   __   __

Numbers: 1   __   __   __   __   __   __   __   __

Names: G   __   __   __   __   __   __   __   __

Numbers: 1   __   __   __   __   __   __   __   __

Names: A   __   __   __   __   __   __   __   __

Numbers: 1   __   __   __   __   __   __   __   __

Seventh Position Pattern II

Seventh Position Pattern II

The Octopiece

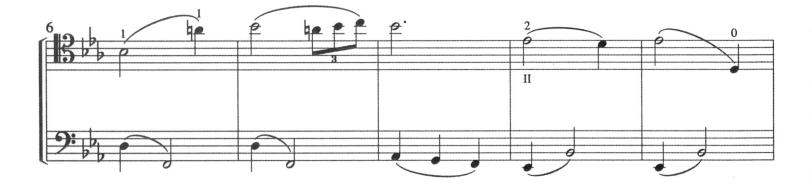

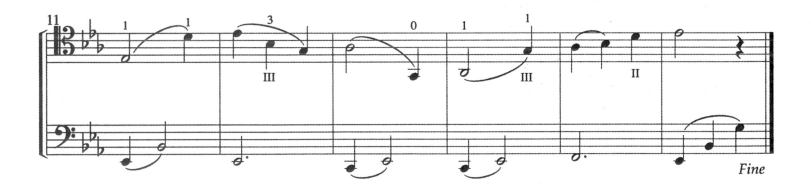

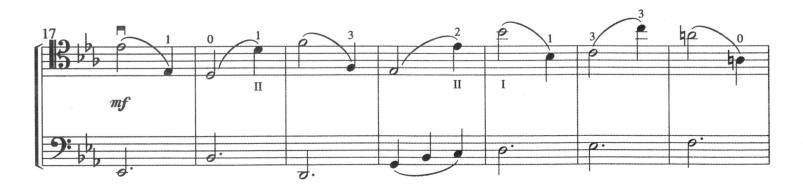

The Octopiece

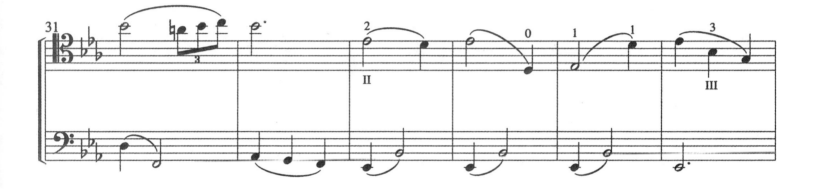

D. C. al Fine

Jig

Seventh Position Pattern III

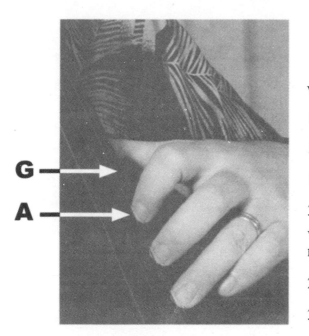

G →
A →

Geography Quiz

Your 1st finger is on A on the A-string.
Answer the following questions:

What note will be played by:

1 on the D-string? _____

1 on the G-string? _____

1 on the C-string? _____

3 on the A-string? _____

What is another
name for that note? _____

2 on the D-string? _____

3 on the G-string? _____

What finger will you use to play:

B on the A-string? _____

E on the D-string? _____

A on the G-string? _____

E on the C-string? _____

F♯ on the D-string? _____

D on the C-string? _____

C♯ on the A-string? _____

Names and Numbers

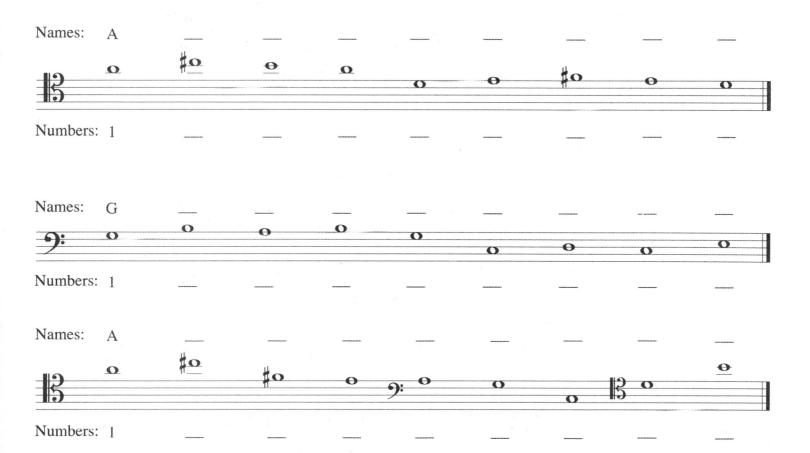

Seventh Position Pattern III

Seventh Position Pattern III

Laissez Les Bons Temps Rouler

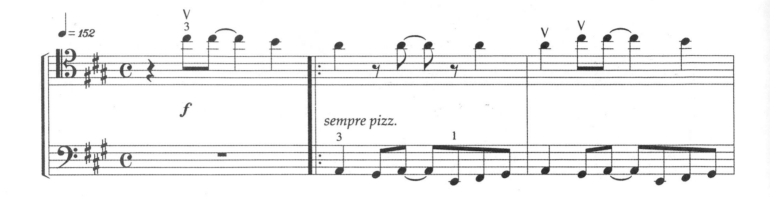

(Good + Rag) x Time

Fine

D. C. al Fine

Arietta

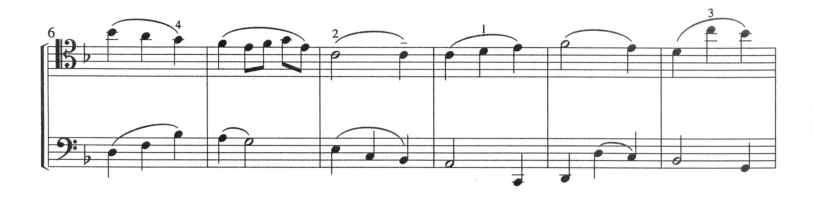

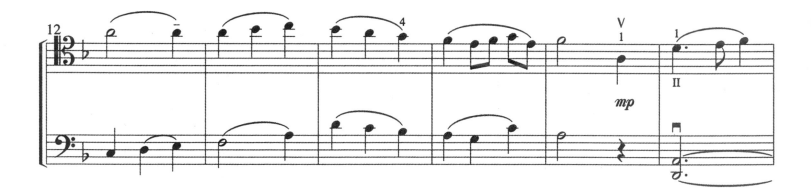

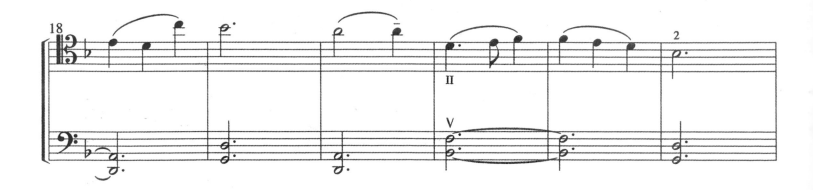

Arietta

Cello Baby Boogie

Cello Baby Boogie

Metal Cellos

Metal Cellos

Time Management Blues

Fanfare

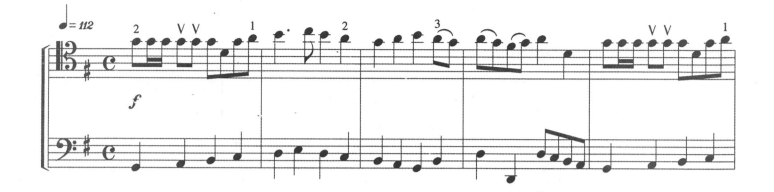

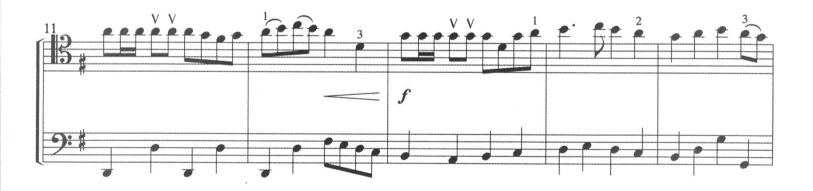

Surfing Cellos

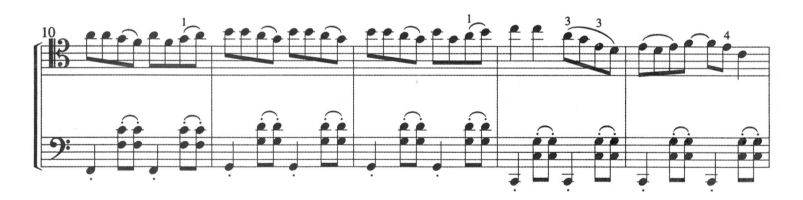

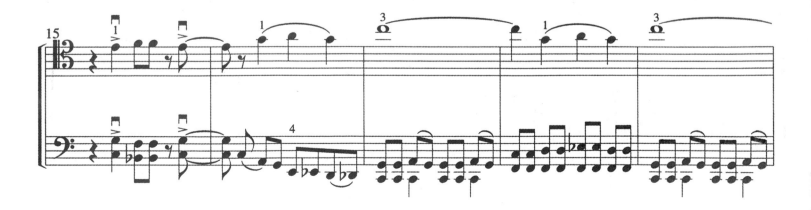

Surfing Cellos

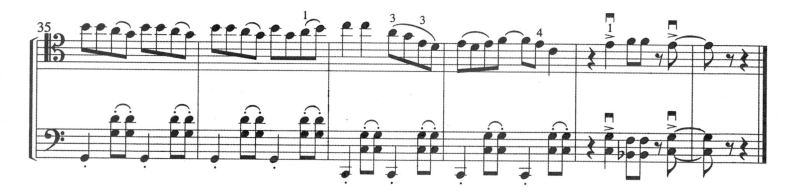

Malagueña

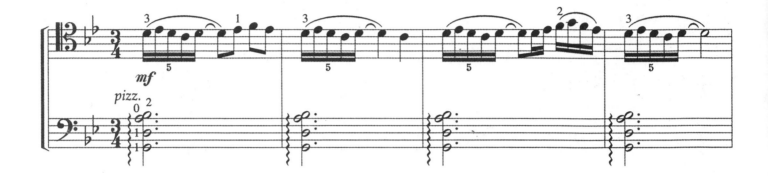

Malagueña

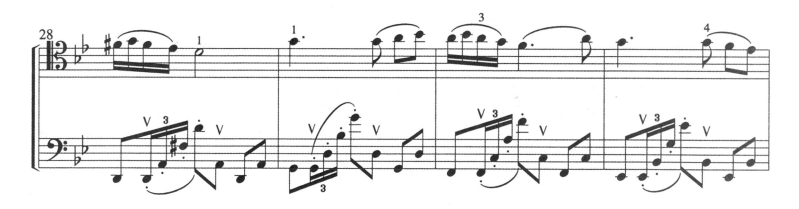

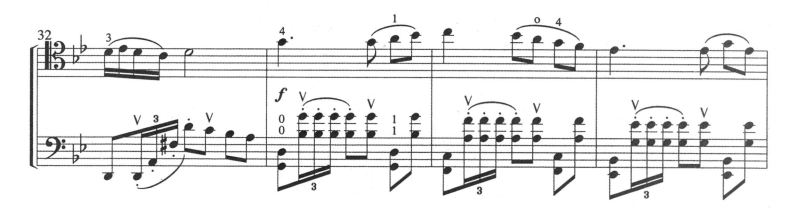

Malagueña

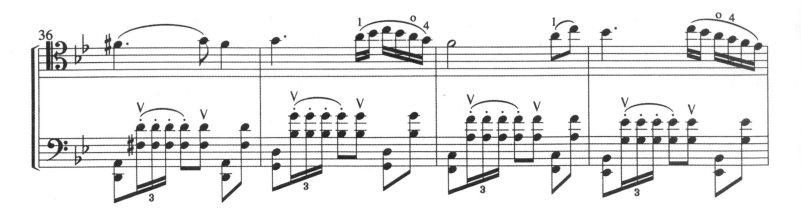

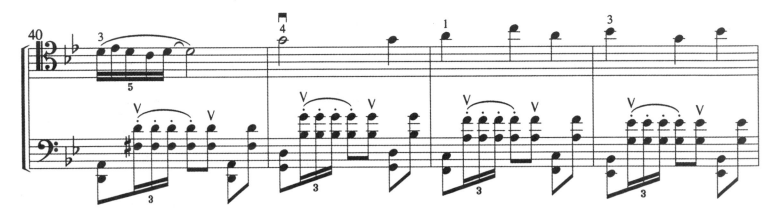

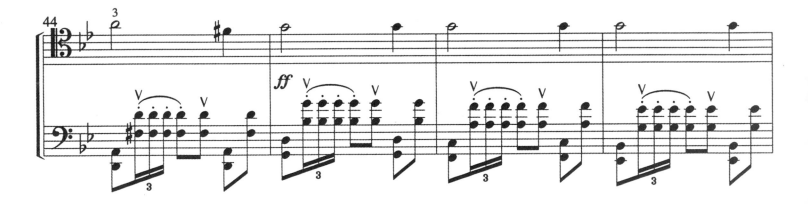

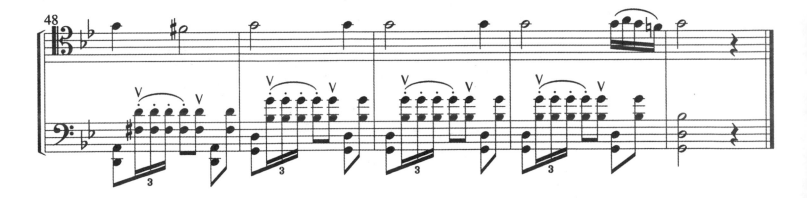

Jumping Flea

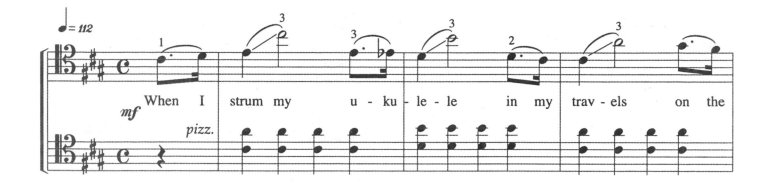

Jumping Flea

hair. There are man - y great teach-ers here at Juil - liard, but there's

no one to teach the u - ku - le - le. So that means that

now I have to play my cel - lo all day and I

al - most nev - er get to play my u - ku - le - le. When I

There are

Jumping Flea

Bariolage Barrage

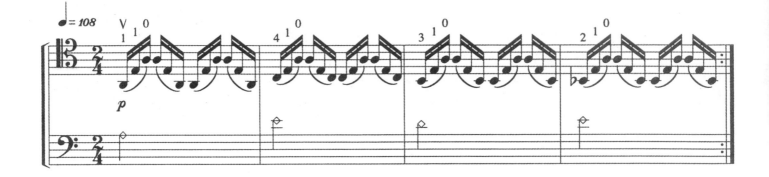

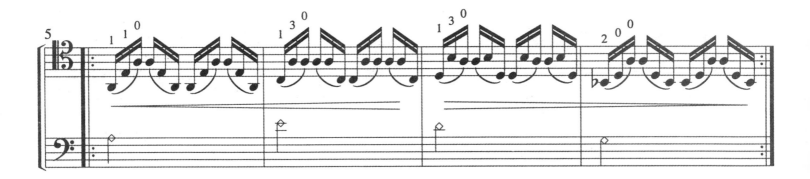

Bariolage Barrage

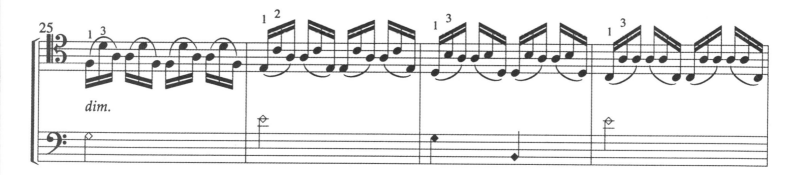

Bariolage Barrage

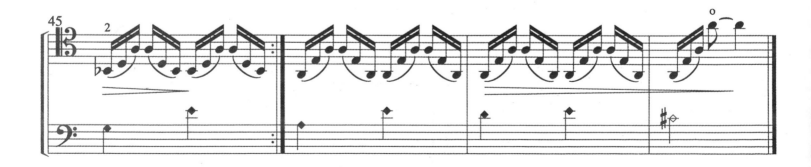